Listening to Dancing

Thanks are due to the editors of the following publications in which some of these poems have appeared:
Bête Noire, *Critical Quarterly*, *First Draft*, *Ms.* (USA), *Pearl* (USA), *Poetry Wales*, *Quadrant* (Australia), *Scratch*, *Second Draft*, *Sheaf*, *Sheffield Thursday*, *Slow Dancer Magazine*, *Sunk Island Review*, *Sycamore Review* (USA), *The Echo Room*, *The North*, *The Rialto*, *The Wide Skirt*, *Verse*

Previous publications:

Listening to Dancing (Slow Dancer, 1989) – out of print
Raw (The Wide Skirt Press, 1990) – out of print
Nobody Move (Slow Dancer, 1992)

Listening to Dancing

Janet Fisher

Smith/Doorstop Books

Published 1996 by
Smith/Doorstop Books
The Poetry Business
The Studio
Byram Arcade
Westgate
Huddersfield HD1 1ND

ISBN   1 869961 58 7

British Library Cataloguing-in-Publication Data. A catalogue
record for this book is available from the British Library.

Typeset at The Poetry Business
Printed by Peepal Tree, Leeds
Cover by blue door design, Heckmondwike

Distributed by Password (Books) Ltd.,
23 New Mount Street, Manchester M4 4DE

The Poetry Business gratefully acknowledges the help of
Kirklees Metropolitan Council and Yorkshire & Humberside
Arts.

Cover photo by Claire McNamee

Cover illustration: 'Dessin de Christian Bérard
pour "Cotillon"'.

Cotillon: a petticoat, or a dance for eight people.

CONTENTS

From Lakeland

> *'Do not interfere with this lifebelt,*
> *a life may depend on it.'* – Sign on empty stand, Grasmere

1.

A duck on a rock speaks truth to the multitude.
Beyond the bright familiar grasses
two people are in a boat – a memory of itself:
two people in a boat on a lake snapping each other.
You had that funny red jumper on.

Across the high bank a woodpecker hammers
through air so still all sound is held, given back.

2.

My moving hand and several sets
of fingers echo in the mirror
on the baize desk, its distorting bevel.
In the drawer is a prayer on yellow paper.
The voices of sheep are the cries
of the old in starchy beds. 'Prayer
is a room you can always go to':
a boudoir, a soup kitchen.

The story outline
Life as preface (not death or heaven, waiting):
    on the move/park up at friends/they've had this before/
                                   sink deeper;
    the broken phone, pen-punched (always the Great
                               Communicator);
    Straw: on the floor, in her hair, in the wind, clutching at;
    Wise lined faces (give her younger men, softskinned, abrupt)

    June bugs banging on windows, losing their legs.

Voice to hang it on? - letters (dramatic irony), first person,
                              third person, God.

She's found someone to take her in.

What is the good of this
unless it's good?

3.
From the tribal meeting place high in the hills
where I pick up a stone for a friend who collects them
I take the winding road past four white skeletons
of beech trees to the church of St John of Jerusalem.
Feeling some dedication is called for here,
embarrassed, hoping they're anonymous enough,
I write some names in the book of prayer.

4.
The letter
'Next time you pass a phone box
or order lunch or join a queue
to see where it's heading, think of me,
whether you are my friend or not.
I can't talk of debit and credit.
You take what you want.

'And should you need
to write a poem to a friend,
next time do it,
do it to their face. I need
to tell you I love you
to find out if I do. I lifted that
from somewhere.
But it will do. For you.'

5.
Allonby, home of the bacon sandwich,
the fossil, the shush of the sea. Horses
gallop, turn, gallop. A wind gets up.
A hard drive back on the coast road
to my pale green room, moth still stuck
in the tooth glass, and the endless packing
of things not worn or worn too often.

Listening to Dancing

I was born after the blitz, when things felt easier,
before his posting. Too young to miss him,
I cried at the top of the stairs
the day a wooden box arrived from Africa,
full of ebony, coconuts and carved heads,
unhallmarked gold. The snow was bad that year.

When he returned he brought me strange dolls,
beaded bags, elephants. I played politely,
listening to dancing on the wireless,
Gathering Peascods, pretending to be eight people.
At my baptism I was dragged out screaming
because my painted white shoes were squeezing my toes.

In damp hedgerows I found violets, the scented kind,
celandine, cuckoo pint, but my own secret places
were invisible, my inquisitive fingers smelt of fishpaste,
like sandwiches for Sunday tea. Some winter evenings,
my mother at church, he made me cocoa
so strong and sweet I could hardly drink it.

It Depends on Your Point of View

That Christmas she cried a lot in secret,
shouted at the wrong people: her best friends,
the postman. Visitors drank her whisky, laughed
at her jokes, pretended not to notice:
it was Santa Claus all over again.
Then her leg swelled up so she couldn't walk.
She lay on the sofa contemplating interesting facts:
that a whale has a six foot penis yet is singularly
unattractive; that meadowsweet is anti-inflammatory
and an alternative to aspirin; that soap operas
confront the burning issues of our time.

'Don't Mention It'

He brings the logs in, holding them like children
on the crook of his arm, stacks the basket,
dusts his hands on his jeans. 'That's the last,
beech or oak, I don't know. Should burn well.'
I stay in my chair, not looking at his rolled-up sleeves,
the way his shirt's not quite tucked in at the back.
The fire falls, reveals its centre.

He kneels, places a log across the coals.
'That'll see the night out.' 'Thanks. It's kind of you.'
'What are neighbours for?' We stand up, shake hands.
His is calloused, hard. I offer a drink.
'Better not, they'll be expecting me.' The night air
has scented his skin. 'Oh, just for half an hour,
to watch the fire. I'm not sure that log will catch.'

Platonic

With you among the crowd who sit ears pricked,
watchful and dumb as dogs – just you, knowing
what it is I want from you, want to give you,
alone in the little park, its plants in stiff rows,
waiting for summer to bring them to bloom

(the natural world comes to this in the end)
the evening air is scented with opportunity,
but between us the questions hang like swords.
Just your hand in the small of my back is enough
to bring me to the point you put your finger on every time.

By the Pump Dry-Eyed

           across from two men and a boy,
flaunt it, written in their eyes,
the sun, the diet, giving her that lightness,
that looseness of hip enough to feel the bite

of lewd stares, and old enough to appreciate it.
Perhaps they were only dozing by the wrenches,
heavy lids drowsy with heat not lust;
perhaps they were merely licking

the dust from their lips. Giddy with fumes,
a shimmer of petrol blurring her gaze,
she slots the pipe and fishes for credit,
pockets the flimsy to show her husband.

Come Clean

on feelings, smash hits, pornography,
the best way from A to B, who left
the window open, who let the plant die,
the love of a lifetime, picking bones

and pulling wishbones. Nothing passes
her lips without a fight. The radio
in the next room, the click of knives.
The boiler blurts on. She has discovered

a talent for lying, she lives it,
her DNA is refurbished with lies.
Truth is no longer a beacon,
its dazzle no longer hurts her eyes.

She sneezes. Even her sneeze is a lie.
She tells the truth always
and it is a lie, the worst kind,
embedded, like the last pin in a new shirt.

Journey's End

Getting up at half six
I drove off for Dewsbury in the fog
having had two slices of toast and
difficulty in getting my child to nursery.

Negotiating the middle lane in an
ever increasing sense of insecurity
I was hemmed in by an articulated lorry
carrying car axles from Dusseldorf to Newcastle,

causing me unfortunately to miss my junction
so that, abandoned in a stream of traffic,
I hopefully flashed my lights at the XR3i in front and
he having returned my signal drew in at the nearest service station.

Needing a shoulder to cry on I sat with him
on a grassy bank overlooking the Happy Eater and when
he put his hand up my skirt and nibbled my ear
life had never been sweeter.

Having renegotiated the carriageway upon
which as it happened the traffic was now thinning out
I found it by a judicious use of the accelerator
possible to get to work only twenty seven minutes late.

Pateley Bridge

She paid for lunch. She did not mind,
they would eat well for a time
on the cheeses and wines she brought.
I am very hungry, she thought,
I will not regret it. So
she fetched rolls, Brie, Bresse Bleu,
Ribblesdale and tasty Lancs,
and two bottles of Piesporter.

They ate by a river, trailing their feet in the water.
That night she gratefully accepted his thanks.

Moments of Reprieve

The day is warming up
and we've hit the motorway.

Dennis the Menace wonders how long
a human can last without food.
Ishtar at the seven gates slides past
the rolls and crisps, misses the cooling towers,
and has her seven magical defences removed,
stands naked in the underworld.
The kids nick all the red M&Ms
and Leicestershire holds the morning
in the palm of its hand.

The picnic area inside the Science Museum
is bordered by the flowers of technology.
I lay with you once under the highbeamed
atmospheric engine, gazing at the planetary dome
in our silver asbestos fire suits
which didn't hinder our mobility,
next to the spacecraft which had carried
three men round the moon.

In Covent Garden the streets are paved with loaves,
apple cores in the gutter. I offered you
apples, but you preferred something softer,
grapes, say, or oranges.

The shops are full of poems
by people I have heard of and don't know.

The city opens its night arms to me again,
a different world from the one I've grown to.
A child in my warm lap, heavy as stone,
all the way home I trace the companionable moon.

Freesias

The valentine from the man she
eventually married said
what more do you want – blood?
but nothing from the man who'd taken her
to the ball, had brought her freesias
for her dress, had fingered her gently
in front of his gas fire as the man
she eventually married burst in
to borrow a match, and stood there.

Raw

He did not understand her rage.
Food was short and he had contacts,
had butchered well during the war,
the colonel still asked for his best cuts,
housewives on points queued for his sausages,
begged for mince under the counter,

      but shut in his cold room
he sliced and jointed, cleaving lambs
from neck to crotch, his heart bleeding,
and he posted her yielding parcels
in leaking greaseproof of kidney, top rump,
plump breasts, which the postman left
by the back entry

        till one hot Thursday after closing
he crept round, slipped through her letter box
slices of liver thick and damp, and waited
as summoned by the clatter she stood rigid
at the red lipped succulence kissing her toes.

An Offal Tale

He offers her
heart, belly, bone.
He's fifty, the balloons declare it
and the flush on his cheeks
is love or whisky, the veins in his arms
swollen with embarrassment.

She takes his parcels, lays them
in her basket with the eggs and cream
she has enticed from the dairyman.
Shopping is what she is good at.
Her eyes promise rich stock, stews, trifles;
her freezer and microwave render
nothing but prepack and quickchill.

Notes for a Part Work

1. From the vestry window he sees her getting into the taxi. She isn't going to her sister's as the note says. The next thing they hear, she's flown to New York with all the money her father left her and an older man who is 67. This is true.

2. Anyhow, she prefers older men. She is 36.

3. Scientists say

4. light is a wave or a particle but not both. Thus she will come back or she won't; she will spend the twenty grand or she won't; she will miss the kids or she won't. This is not determined.

5. Our days number us, tyranny of streams and mirrors.

6. She is a bird drugged by the glamour of his wrinkled eyes.

7. She is also the snake pinned to the grass in the cleft of the hunter's stick.

8. She is also the cruel dreamer who when she wakes makes the world disappear.

9. One day she may return, only to leave again when the children are older.

10. Her sister says she will become a prostitute on the streets of New York and will die of Aids. This is a dream.

11. Her husband is a rector and keeps up appearances. The children must be told. They must also attend church in their best suits. This is determined.

The Snarling Wife Answers Back

'a snarling wife on the balustrade is more
than a man can bear' – from 'they, all of them, know'
by Charles Bukowski

ask the radio
ask the vacuum cleaner
ask the last of the vodka
ask the woman on a bicycle
ask the clothes basket, the window cleaner
ask the last chance
ask the girl on the ledge
ask the person on the other end
ask the floozie in the jaccuzzi (every city has one)
ask the holiday snapshot
ask the man who eats shit, the man who talks shit,
                              the man who is shit
ask the fillibusterer
ask the dead leader
ask the double yellow
ask the flatearther, the ansafone
ask the child abuser, the money launderer
ask the clerk down the social
ask the final solution
ask the man in the patrol car
ask the woman by the lamppost
ask the man with a pickaxe
ask the aborted foetus
ask the enema, the spinal tap, Karpowski's sarcoma,
ask the ball out of play
ask the egg on your face
ask the hangover, the sugar rush, the caffeine high
ask the lump in the sofa
ask the gutting knife
ask the body image
ask the man with a career structure
ask the woman with a spreadsheet
ask dogs in space
ask the cellulite
ask a Kalashnikov

ask the childbearing hips
ask rabbits with tears in their eyes
ask the broken reed
ask the unfrocked priest
ask the nymphet
ask the lying bastard, the bounced cheque
ask the twist in the tail
ask the elephant foot umbrella stand
ask the zen of the art of the dead fish
ask the best of a bad job
ask the jailer, the poacher, the wicket keeper
ask the woman in the zimmer frame
ask the nuclear scientist
ask the hostage, the terrorist
ask the traffic cone, the airbag, the windbag

and they will tell you, oh how they will
tell you in no uncertain terms
that a man caught with his trousers down
deserves a thistle up his arse.

The New Men

Romanoffs and dinosaurs are staging a comeback.
The cloned dead could soon be in our streets
poking their necks through the windows

of the Winter Palace, claiming we got it wrong
again. The start of another era, the overlapping
strata like Russian cake sticky with honey.

I mean, when my friend had her abortion
on her lover's birthday I took her flowers,
helped feed the toddler. Everyone held hands

in '68 and shrugged off the war but it carried on
anyway somewhere or other. What can you do?
There are always women crying in dressing gowns.

I heard you can get an NVQ in housework
and homemaking. Man management.
That's the one. Easy.

House Music

It's no go the sacred stones, it's no go the mushroom,
All we want is a piece of cake and a roll-up in the front room.
Their evening skirts are St. Laurent, their petticoats Janet Reger,
They buy shampoo from Body Shop
                            but their knickers are made of leather.

Ally McAllister bought a bike, polished the chrome like silver,
Went a ton with his girl on the back, hit a bus and killed her.
Sharon O'Docherty shaved her head, painted the stubble purple,
Danced the dance of the seven veils and shocked
                            the Mayor of Mirfield.

It's no go the YTS, it's no go the Social,
All we want is a Newky Brown and keep our place in the dole queue.

Garry Bishop hadn't a job, thought he'd join the Army,
Six months marching on Salisbury plain, brains blown out in Derry.
His brother Steven did the same, was shot in the Territorials,
Now he's in a Cheshire Home painting war memorials.

It's no go the party plan, it's no go the video,
All we want is a pair of Docs and a front seat at the road show,
It's no go a fortnight's sun, it's no go Marbella,
All we want is a pat on the back to prove we're not a failure.

Lara Jones was twelve years old, didn't really look it,
Had a kid one Friday night and left it in a bucket.
Auntie Vi at the Halloween hop couldn't stop herself screaming,
Woke up next day with the man next door,
                            life took on a new meaning.

It's no go the Prince's Trust, it's no go Malvinas,
It's no go the enterprise grant or a pair of patched Pacinos.
It's no go the data base, it's no go the spread sheet,
Stick your head in a plastic bag and listen to your heart beat.

It's no go, my sweetie pie, it's no go, my darling,
put the benefit in the bank, you won't get change from a farthing.
The grass is greener wherever you look, and never trust the punters,
But if you sit on the bloody fence you get the bloody splinters.

25

Jocasta

And the first time I saw him
like the world after rain,
the old man dead and the young man standing there,
his hair still damp, shrugging
the wet cloak from his shoulders.

Waking from fever, my throat aching,
my body clear as spring water,
head light with a bright intensity like wire,
like diamond. And his eyes,
blue as the Aegean, as lightning.

He rubbed his hands down his thighs
wiping off dirt and blood.
It had been a long ride.
I ordered water but I was there first,
unloosing his sandals, drying his wounded foot
on my new dress. My heart drowning.

We made him our king,
my king. Can you doubt it?

That was twenty years ago; he is as old
as I was then, our children grown.
But it's over. I'm finished with guilt and grief.
I will not give Heaven that satisfaction.
His reddened eyes have healed, his scars hardened.
Someone else must cry for him. My throat is dry.

Trophy

From the bedroom window she watches him
hop from car to door in purple pants, no shoes.
Owls had woken her. She guesses he'd left
the keys in the car or heard a lion
escape into a nearby garden.
It's barely dawn.

The bed's a fourposter, reproduction. She pretends
she's Marie Antoinette. The tumbrils are waiting.
A guard is at the door. He smells of cheese.
His rough burlap brushes her peachy skin.
He drags her into the street. Her pearls,
lily white under the moon, roll down the gutter.
She cries, but that won't save her.
She offers her treasures. They snatch them
and get her anyway. Her heart shifts
at the wrong she has done them.

When he comes in, shivering,
she bathes the long scratches on his back
and calls him her hero, her mercenary.

In Touch

You get up early, put flowers in my room
before I arrive, foot on the pedal up the A1
into grey clouds, an opening light over the hills.
It will rain, won't rain, hangs in the air.
So what if it does, we go well back,
we can take the odd storm. Your house
is big enough for sofas; we'll curl up
and talk about what we've read, haven't read,
what we remember. The men in the case
can join the queue.
                              It's OK being in touch
with ourselves, each other. Letters, no letters
over the years, a card or two. They used to ask
if we were twins: same dark hair. But does it end
there? I wanted to live with you then.
At our age the danger's to stop exploring,
you with your Saturn in Libra tipping the scales,
me Moon in Aquarius weeping
over the fortunes of the not quite there yet.
                              Supper's good, it always is
when you're around, nothing's too much
trouble. Baked squash, greens frizzled in butter
and almonds. The courses never stop coming.
At last the caviar, special import, just a taste
salt and sharp on the tongue, the iced vodka
downed in one sets us coughing and laughing.

Iron Age

Nitty gritty under my nails, round the quick,
my moons black. These crumbs
were once a woman's comb, her cup,

her best necklet. I scrub and scrape.
The tent is cold; through the flaps
clouds scud, the moon like a sniper

bobs out and back. I trawl the careful mounds,
a graverobber, rubbing my fingers in it.
All night the tarps bang in the wind.

Three thousand years is irrelevant:
she had backache, slapped
her kids, got up swearing at dawn.

Axe heads and barley husks, turd, bones,
to be bagged and catalogued, buried
in the museums I spend my life in.

The Elder Son

'The pigs stuck out their little feet and snored'
       – from 'The Prodigal' by Elizabeth Bishop

He stuffed himself with the pickings, sweet cuts
off the back of the joint, and spuds melting in gravy,
licking his fingers took over the farm, his father crazy
and mother under the table. He grew fat on his debts,
littered the pig pens with sweets and crisp packets ,
his belly ready to farrow, but he drove cows to market
and fetched the best price. Each night, feet flat
on the verges, he fixed his sights onto the tumbling stars
through a narrow glass, fighting the sense of ambush
when he entered a room, of papers thrust into drawers .
The maps in his head turned to plans in his pocket.
Stick at it, all this would be his in a few years.
He had struck the rock and brought forth living waters.
Mobile clamped to his ear he listened for the rush.

As he wrestled the calf from its mother, the bristling nap
like a prayer mat under his palm, the low moans
when she turned her wild eyes at him were not hers alone.
The calf too spread out its gangly legs and griped
till the warm bottle he took from his jacket soothed it.
Once locked in its wooden pen, he shook his head
but that was the price of milk: use it or lose it.
'You can't eat pigshit, cows are our living.' His veal
was the best in the county; his reputation, they said,
grew with his appetite. One day he was bringing it tasters
when his father, by the gate as usual scanning the horizon,
started to run to the speck on the far pasture,
arms wide; and he knife in hand strode to the pen,
slit the throat and flayed the flesh for the welcome meal.

Existentialist

Behind drawn curtains in reflecting shades
he sits and strums:

the reek of spitted pig in cafe windows;
down by the Seine cheap prints for sale. He found
a Degas once, 500 francs, a dancer bending
in a small dusty square. Geraniums.

The Louvre was disappointing though,
the Mona Lisa tucked up behind crowds, guards,
the mirror only of his own small smile.
Moustache and beret were imaginary.

The city breathed cheap wine, Gitanes, couscous,
hump-backed buses where in felt skirts curling
round their thighs the girls waved, kissed, descended
and descended the steps of Pigalle into the Metro night.

A stinking hole, a straw bed, dawn
from a cold gable across red roofs,
hearing the barrowmen hawk in the gutter
their golden onions.

Amy

From her chair by the fire she sees legs,
pram wheels, footballs, the top of the stone
wall round the Chapel of Rest. On fine days
she washes her windows with a broom,

reaching down. She has no letterbox,
collects her mail from the undertakers.
They're old friends. On the piano
are photos, vases, dried flowers,

in her drawer the folded white
handkerchief she saves for funerals.

Forty Years

I've been here, thistles and barbed wire,
dragging the ground. In spring I pull the tops
of nettles for soup, staring into the sun.
Later it's elderberries, the wine
in plastic buckets behind the sofa.
I can't pull the plug on it, somehow,
I can't see the end of it. There's gold
in the dandelions, they'll do when the bread runs out.

Others come in their vans and trailers,
dressed in rags, hair all colours.
They think I'm one of them, invite me in
for a smoke. I don't go, it's not for me.
They have babies, bikes, goats. They don't eat meat,
but I saw one kill a hare with his bare hands.
Ask no questions.

I don't mind. But the farmer's cut the trees,
the hedges. They bring papers,
wave them in my face. I say nothing.
They promise me a flat, hot dinners.

Ah, but a rabbit kicks hard long after it's dead.
And I think of him trudging home at sunset,
dog-tired, shotgun broken across his arm.
His eyes dark, heavy. The bruised, stiffening bodies
tipped out over the scullery floor.

Satyr

I'm washed up with it all.
Psychiatrists, what do they know?
Thirty women a night,
they call you a closet gay.
I'd like to see them try it.

Mind you, the past twenty years,
every one's at it. Most don't know
what it means; it's all late shows,
young men in shaggy cardigans
being rude in a witty way.
They don't appreciate my status.
I'm even a medical condition.

I'm on the wagon, to tell you the truth.
No more bits of hot stuff lining up
like cold takeaways. I'm more worried
about getting my hind legs stuck
in the escalator, or treading in bubblegum
that some young layabout
who five years ago I'd have had
down a back alley in thirty seconds
has spat out on the Mall floor.

I yearn sometimes for streams and groves.
But the Mall's my big thing these days.
I comb my thighs and polish my hooves
to a dazzle, then I fly down the avenues
under the mirror balls. Twinkle toes,
they call me. The last of the big benders.

The Complete Works

Pink edges damp with coffee spilled
while dozing off in a double seminar
on the late plays, a present from an aunt
for passing his A levels, not quite the thing
for a university, more at home in a Doncaster
boarding house, and not much good on notes.
Weighty stuff with a hollow centre
for hiding guns, secrets, words.

I Bruise Easily

The day I went to Blackpool
on the train through Manchester
the woman stuck a needle up me for a fiver
and I came back the same day, bleeding,
and that night on the floor it came out, a girl,

but that was just the second. The first
when I still thought babies came out of your button
I drank a cup of washing soda, which burnt
my stomach, made me sick, and then
there was the diarrhoea, the blood,

though there may have been no connection.
And later in Ireland during the war,
still the same man, I brought it on myself
humping bags of coal because Wendy aged three
was all I could cope with at the time.

We had four kids, and then I married him,
but he still went with the others, Pakis, blacks,
and later little girls he paid for buggery
though I never heard it called that before –
that was worth more than a year in Armley.

But my father, who abused me before I was born
by giving me syphilis, blinding me by ten,
(no penicillin, eyes injected
three times a day till the sight returned
by God's grace, not the doctors'),

well, he wasn't a bad man, he'd only one arm,
would stand in our mother's way when
mad with disease she beat us, starved us,
forced us out so we slept in the back toilets
or crept into cars.

And the one I live with now, my youngest,
in a house full of miniatures and statuettes –
him and his boyfriend, they want me in a Home;
he beats me when he's had a skinful
and certainly if he knew I'd been talking to you.

A Life

He forced his way into it, a near shave.
The strawberry mark on his neck, the thick tongue:
the midwife gave thumbs down as she left by the back gate
to Mrs B next door peering behind curtains.
They're past it, must have been an old packet,
she muttered, wheeling her bike down the side.

He didn't walk till three. Once, stood at the bath side
he ate a bar of soap and half a tube of Colgate
while his father was having a shit and a shave,
blew minty bubbles through the open end of the packet
and his dad thought he was fitting, shoved a flannel over his tongue,
parcelled his body tight in the shower curtains,

cut his foot on his razor, now knowing for certain
the lad would be always on the outside,
always last to be picked for the team; and his tongue
stuck to his mouth. He called him a young shaver,
washed him, belted him tight to the safety gate,
warned his mother mustn't know or they'd both catch a packet.

They scraped and saved for private school, but had to pack it
in. Was it his refusal to work, keep clean, shave,
or his knowledge of markets and his small deals on the side?
Denied escape, he gave them the rough edge of his tongue,
spent his teens in his room screaming, climbing the curtains.
He plotted possibilities, routes to the other side of the gate.

At 18 he cut and ran to a basement in Margate.
Its separate entrance was worth a packet;
though the mould glowed in the dark he didn't need curtains.
He built up his contacts, got rich, even put a bit aside.
Each night in his white trilby, a splash of aftershave,
a little something dissolved on the back of the tongue,

he would wink at himself in the mirror, his tongue
flicking his lips like a cat's, slip behind curtains
at the back of cafés, dispensing his small packets

like a teacher with pencils, closing the floodgate
on conscience. He fixed it himself, cutting down the side
with a clear eye, a sharp blade, a clean shave.

Caught, strip searched, head shaved, in a room without curtains,
names, dates, on the tip of his tongue. Then they slammed the gate.
And two people grieved a packet, the rest put it to one side.

Is the First Day of the Rest of Your Life

And it's back to learning new ways to breathe,
talk, whistling up letters on a green screen.
Dear mum today they got me writing a

His mates wheel him down the pub. They play brag.
He still laughs when they tell him their latest –
tipping their Chinese over some wanker.
When he wants to raise he can nod his head.

He has a special gadget just to turn
the pages of his favourite paper.
But it's all in the mind. He wakes up, his
nose itches. Jesus. Yes, my son, today

Way Way

She slept in the afternoons
before they all came home,
on the sofa by the gas fire
with duvet, hot water bottle, codeine.
Once, the early setting sun in her eyes
half woke her and she was floating
above the sofa, dizzy with fumes.
A strong wind rushed over her body
like a river; her limbs shook. 'Christ save me!'
There was her eldest kneeling beside her:
'We had to give him back,
we had to give him back.'
But she knew this wasn't true,
it just wasn't true: his baby
lost in long grass or whipped off
by women in anoraks and Fiestas
yelling there was no way this family
could look after a baby, no way.

Day Trip

In '67, some weeks after the Israelis
had kicked the shit out of the Arabs,
I crossed Belgium with my friend Shirley
heading for the Conference of Christians
and Jews in Strasbourg, where they stuff
geese for their livers. I met an anti-
Zionist called Martin with a degree
in politics who made mincemeat
out of people's arguments and we went on
odd visits – the Cathedral spire is completely
open at the top, after two bottles of Pinot Blanc
no joke – and to the local camp, the only one
they built in France apparently where I stood
in the porcelain room they used for the gassings
surprised it was so small.

Fifty Years On

it's Quiz Night at the Chamberlain Arms and Frank
has written the questions himself this time.
Jane, Irma and I, drinking ginger wine, drying up
on England captains and the length of snooker tables,

squeeze fragments of gossip into the gaps.
The Vicar has been asked to bless the Scout
Hut as a rates dodge, it's part of the job
like praying for the dead and always smiling,

but Jane comparing the Cubs to Hitler Youth is probably
tactless: Irma's father was in the Luftwaffe,
a P.O.W. who stayed on. Irma hates Poles
and Communists. We're into the second half and Frank

is hotting up the humour. Which United player is
a German newspaper? Zy Tung? Dee Velt? The answer
is Gerry Daley, Jane declares it's racist and Irma
pinks up. Later over coffee she pounces on my

Tradascantia. Do let me have a piece of your
Wandering Jew, she exclaims, waving the scissors.

The Old Ghetto, Krakow

They don't speak English but understand
when we say we're not Jewish, lend
the men skullcaps anyway, which don't fit.
The guided tour is a kind of dumb show.
The synagogue has that musty smell
and the graveyard is like any other.

Down the road the whitewashed museum
is lighter and airier, displaying the last
of Jewish craft in this country: hangings,
plates, Passover loaves, a few
photos of people running for trains,
belongings scattered in the street.

Camp

If you do not have a towel
you will be punished.
You clench it in your knees when you wash.
If you put it down it will vanish.
If you do not wash you will be punished.

You carry your hunger everywhere,
a dead animal on your back.
You cannot put it down
not even for a second.

In the Bar

After two vodkas, local measure, Poland
shifts about a bit. A habit of history.
There's a man here I've seen before
in corner bars all over Europe,
flight bag slung on one shoulder,
jingling change in different currencies.
Travellers' tales: I've heard them,
but it's always news, this tang of other places,
like the authentic vodka I'll buy tomorrow
for the journey home, local price.

Amsterdam

Everything else is going strong. Sex
in the streets, ladies naked under fun furs,
boys pursing their lips. I'm careless

of trams clipping corners like scissors
round a seam; on the lemon-slice bridges
cyclists ring bells, shout as if they own me.

I've raged all day, my head is in orbit.
In the restaurant the waiter crouches,
sit-on-a-happy-face badge pinned

to his bottom, gently explaining the menu.
I play sleeping lions like a child at a party.
The chef's choice is springbok, straight

off the savannah, tender, with apple sauce.
Through the hotel's open window,
the fountain glassy in the trembling half light,

smoke rises like laughter.
I have cut my hand tripping on a tramline;
my new jacket seeps blood into a cup of water.

Pearls

The Archangel bears down from his pinnacle,
his flaming sword ravaging the pagan,
the tourist, sellers of novelty monks
and snow scenes of Mont St Michel.

Seven evenings watching sunsets beyond the islands:
the chrysanthemum, the coughdrop, the candyfloss,
the red hot poker, three blank looks.

By Tuesday we yearn for interiors, forests,
anything unconnected with the sea.
We lunch in the garden, the cherry tree
heavy with unformed fruit. The lawn
sprouts mushrooms, but we do not trust them.

A hot afternoon outside the cafe, oysters in boxes,
cheap. They would slip down so easily.
My stomach tightens: the price is too high.

Soaping a flannel I count seven reasons for owning a bidet:
before after after during when right foot left foot.

The bikers get up another chorus of 'Eye of the Tiger'
as France backs off, richer for having met us.

Bedsit

No men, no blacks. This is Handsworth *Wood*.
A rug hides the dust over brown lino ringed
by shifted bed ends; posters are forbidden
on the finger-printed walls. You think of lunch,
but Dad downs the cases too quickly, sets off
back hunched, down the long road. School starts
tomorrow and you don't know what to expect.

Other tenants explain the kitchen, the rotas.
Betty's in business. Miss Bolt teaches Games.
A penny in the meter boils three potatoes.
Afterwards Annie shuffles through to steal
your gas ends. Each night you come back
to a blank wall where you paint tomorrow,
now you know what to expect, with only the Beatles
for company: Eleanor Rigby. Rubber Soul.

Not Knowing the Names of Plants

you study the pictures on the boxes,
pick out stocks, chrysanths, snapdragons,
the strongest and healthiest. Why is it
so hard to choose? Twenty years ago

we ate tough rump and laughed at the waitress
for chilling the house red, at the next couple
for sitting not speaking all evening, not like us.
Last night the tournedos were tender, the claret

chambré and we did not say anything. Today,
our bedding plants tucked in the boot, we drink tea
from flowered cups and a monsoon drums its heels
on the cafe roof begging to be let in.

Before Tea Saturday

we were waiting for the kettle, chatting of this
and that, when a thud like a blown fuse
and a surging hiss from the demijohn
in the corner told us the rhubarb had burst
its bung, was founting sugar and juice
across the counter. Initial fermentation
being long past, we'd thought it had settled down
into a tacit concentration of flavour
to be bottled and savoured later.
But there it was: country champagne all over
the clean washing. The dregs had gone nasty
so we tipped them on the compost,
and next day we stumbled down to breakfast
and the stink in the kitchen, warm and yeasty.

Swedish Wood

Today I went on a long walk and my legs ache,
and I'm sitting in Kath's house listening. I've brought her
eggs and bread, and fruit for the kids. She keeps a test handy
in her knicker drawer: three kids and a broken marriage,

she can't afford not to. Her husband keeps her short
but her lover doesn't. He's into AmDram in a big way.
Yesterday Ray and I bought a chair from IKEA
with wooden arms to lighten the living room,

and we'll buy the three seater when we've the cash
if it's still in stock. Some people buy marriages
to lighten things, give them a feeling
something's happening. But when you get

to this long you're a bit stuck, it takes a heave
to get out of it, and a new chair is a relief, sort of,
like a trip abroad, or your next book. You don't have to talk
to each other if you don't want to. The old one

we'll put on a tip. The springs were gone anyhow.
Kath was married to a tall bearded balding
architect and she now dates a short bearded
balding architect, but he can cook

and he brings her champagne in bed, and the beard
is only while he's playing Fagin anyway.

Performance

She made toast watching Berstein psych
himself up for the Ninth. By the time
he reached the Adagio it was in flames.

Jonathan

French homework due in Tuesday scribbled
in red on the back of the hand not holding
the roller ball slim-line, black ink, he
confidently analyses Macbeth with his
favoured stylistic flourishes and gothic
Js. Bulbous tips of fingers, half moon
nails bitten to the quick, scrape raw
nostrils. Grown six inches in a year,
hair like wire, witty with teachers
when he meets them in the supermarket,
he knows how far he can go, they tell us.

Boy

He's still there, the baby, the little boy
who wouldn't be fed, turned red at spoons, gagged
on junior Heinz, square lumps of carrot

stuck in his gums, gravy down his jumper.
Still there in those pleading eyes like melted
Mars. Sticky. Forget the slaps, the forcefeeds,

the anger driven like bile from a gut
veined god knows where: way back in history
my father's father, the missionary,

had less luck with the Burmese, damn their souls.
And now there's two people in my kitchen
dressed in rags, no job, no money, but hope,

bags of it lifted god knows where
like that Blue Mountain coffee, the Chanel.
I wouldn't buy it and neither did they.

Rip off. And he tells me another tale,
face all innocent like he'd never smoke,
he'd try harder, laughing up his torn sleeve,

behind my back. But it's all right really,
I know him you see, and when he tells me
his sworn secret I knew it anyway.

When you've been that close you never lose it.
Besides which it isn't hard to guess when
she's sick on your carpet every morning,

plus all the glances, the shared smiles. They tease,
they'll have me in a shawl and rocking chair.
Big eyes, big teeth. Eat up, boy, it's your turn.

Summer Pudding

Seven kinds of fruit, and this is the eighth.
Custard chilled in the cellar, her voice clotted
from Craven A or the bonfire she burnt the weeds on,
in slacks when it wasn't fashionable, hoe in hand.
Supper late again as the chickens squawked,
and she fetched eggs in to hardboil,
to have with bread and salt while she read
and sang to me, inventing the tune
but never forgetting the words.
A mad dance and a handclap,
an audience of one was all she needed.

Who, needing no excuse to bake a fruitcake,
wring a bird's neck and pull the guts, roast it
in a tin oven when the rest of the world
ate chops and shop pies, did she think she was?
Piled with books, old stories and the new,
she broke my indifference, banged me up with words.
Too many, or not enough. Fingers in the custard
and a slap, a shout, for my dirty habits. This is it:
the tales my own children now yawn over –
death, revenge, the split spines of romance,
and the late raspberries pulped in.

Smoke

In the street I pick them out:
kipper skin and that dry laugh.

She always lit up on her feet like a navvy,
spilling ash on the housework, but by the tele
she sat and sucked hazels out of wholenut,
wrapped them in her hanky. Her Kensitas
coupons bought me my suitcase for University,
empty now on a wardrobe of old clothes.
She doesn't inhale, said my father,
it's all right. In our wedding photo,
the one of us cutting the cake,
her face almost unrecognisable
stands out from the back of the crowd
like a ghost, laughing.

A Question of Age

You dance in slow motion, in pain, like an insect
short of a leg or two, across the kitchen, your
kitchen now, for a cup to measure rice.

Questions, answers, locked away
like the wills and certificates
in the bedroom drawer next to the book
on sex within marriage (worn red covers
and forward for its time, explaining the value
of masturbation during enforced absences,
that there was no shame to the marital act, indeed,
only pleasure) which I discovered as a child.

You stir the sweet, hot curry
you learnt to love in India sixty years ago
(no good unless you sweat like a pig), drain
rice fluffy as pillows but never soft. She tried
for forty years to cook rice like that.
Now every week, two or three times,
you feast yourself till your eyes smart.

Dependency

He drinks it well diluted, a tumbler a night
in front of Come Dancing or some such trash
to keep his mind in, his stock in trade.

He used to pour me another
– Let her, it's the only way to teach her –
as I cadged cigarettes off my mother.
The only way to learn. Now alone and arthritic
he anoints the body beautiful in his daily shower,
self pity not his strong point, he reckons.
Bells, Grouse, or some brand off the van
no one's heard of, but for his ninetieth,
because the old don't want knick knacks
but things to enjoy while there's time,
a single malt and socks with easy elastic.

A good servant, he tells the nurses,
but a bad master. Chest worse
after his fall, he eases his granite hips
and sues for the nightcap they can't prescribe
while he's still on the antibiotics.
He hopes the pharmacist is Scottish.
His chances doçked, he keeps the ward awake
all night with D.T.s, shouting for Peggy
till he's no longer able to catch his breath.

It's February But

fog and thaw make the garden smell like Christmas.
Crouched on a low chair at midnight, I'm shifting
bills and statements in search of investments
and debtors. There are none. What's here is here:
enough in the bank for a decent cremation,
no flowers, and an empty cottage
we visit tomorrow to clear of novels
and spoons, suits by now holding the shape
of the hangers, shoes well polished, treed,
unworn. Photos and letters were collected
weeks back, to be done something with.

Then, though I've been through it
a dozen times, under some carbons stashed
at the bottom of the file box: an envelope of papers.
Time has slit their creases like a knife; I lay out
the pieces. They're not, as you'd think,
twelve and a half per cent Treasury Stock redeemable
any day now, but their birth certificates: hers, West Ham,
nineteen fourteen, mother Edith, father Samuel,
a journeyman tool maker; his, Mandalay, nineteen-
o-two, illegible not by age but its unknown script,
curly like Celtic runes, and no signature I can make out.

'There are only so many words'

There are only so many words
and I'm stuck with the ones I've got:
lines drawn desperately between roads,
the singing trees, their lost leaves,
rats running from the blaze.

'Dad died yesterday, last week, last year.'
The echoes grow fainter,
footsteps down a corridor,
swing doors and the smell of dinners,
a notice by a phone: if you are lost, ring here.

Gooseflesh

She even meditates on rites of passage,
decides to celebrate, invite the village.
This is the last one before the big one.
Her body has kept up with fashion:
from sixties pill to menopause,
it's all on the women's page of course.
Her swinging belt is notched with stars.

Some things are not on her agenda
but what *did* she want: a wife, a plumber,
cards on the table and cake for breakfast.
Head rules heart and she'll leave feet first,
the last chocolate in the box.
The earth has opened up its plot.
She grows funny plants from the seeds
her son gave her. Calls them weeds.
The face in the bathroom mirror stinks
of character. As she dyes her hair in the sink,
the red stains lurking round the spout
tell her this time they won't wash out.

Dash

Men have come to fix the pebbledash,
fifty years of it, cracked and letting in the rain.
It needed doing, but it's so noisy
and the scaffolding blocks the path.

In the damp May evening I tiptoe
to the foot of the ladder, up the poles
and onto the roof, the chimney, leap
my giant's leap across mills and fields,
mount the TV mast (all 900 feet of it),
grasp at a passing plane, swing
over and out to the moon, the stars,
till I'm sighted by a schoolboy
at his bedroom window with a telescope,
top of the universe and climbing.

Sunspot

Traffic noise there's no escape from
underlies our conversation,
the zip of sellotape. Another present
wrapped for later; wine chilled,
salmon foiled ready for the oven.

My hair darkened at last from grey
after a summer of negotiation,
sun thrusts its wishes on breasts,
gutters across belly and navel,
a gentle embonpoint curving

to cunt and thighs. Sharp shins;
toes deformed from cheap shoes
will not stop me going barefoot.
As afternoon reaches over the roof top,
we put our feet up to watch the weeds.

When I Get There

it doesn't seem like
I've been away too long but
they all stare and comment
how things have changed since,
how much water etc,
how my hair is greyer or shorter
how the ends of my fingers
don't touch the ground now,
how the thoughts in my head
seem to grow from my ears,
how my new coat makes me
like no one I ever was,
how the space I once filled
is now taken by wellwishers,
card carriers, whistle blowers
of all shape and colour of whistle,
and no one knows where I hang my hat:
in the cupboard of course,
next to the signed photo of
and the broken whatsit.

Economy of Style

Squinting she hand sets each mirrored letter,
tightens the quoins, oils the moving parts:
the rubber rollers slip for a fortnight.
Ink spreads like slander, postmarks her forehead
as fingers push back sweat and hair.
She collects remnants of beautiful paper
torn from fly-leaves, found under the counter,
deckled with mould. She heaves and wrenches
the treadle press, her books struggle for air,
each page an achievement, the wooden benches
littered with smudged uneven discards.
Could be worth something in a few years.
    But she already knows the value of words:
    she cannot sell them for what they cost her.

But the Difference

was, she thought, a good woman
looks after others' interests such as grinding
corn, sewing skirts from old curtains,
hunter gathering, whereas a good

poet doesn't give a bugger, stuffs
herself on chocolate and champagne, sucks
dry the gourd of desire, thus releasing
the good poetry locked within. But being

quite well read as well as good she knew
only too clearly the statistics on obesity,
cyrrhosis and hepatitis B and so forewent
these pleasures though not without certain

feelings of regret and moral complacency. But
she had a problem and it was this: the good
man whom she loved, who did not know
she was sacrificing good poetry for good

womanhood, who sat up late each evening
in their clean kitchen wrapped in a warm
scarf, writing his memoirs, unaware
of what he had nearly missed.

Janet Fisher was born in Birmingham during the war, and grew up in the North Oxfordshire countryside. She lived in London for twelve years before moving with her family to West Yorkshire in 1978. She is co-director of The Poetry Business.

Smith/Doorstop Books

publish books, cassettes
and pamphlets by

Moniza Alvi
Simon Armitage
Sujata Bhatt
Liz Cashdan
Julia Casterton
Linda Chase
Debjani Chatterjee
Bob Cooper
Julia Copus
Tim Cumming
Duncan Curry
Peter Daniels
Carol Ann Duffy
Janet Fisher
Anna Fissler
Katherine Frost
John Harvey
Jo Haslam
Geoff Hattersley
Jeanette Hattersley

Keith Jafrate
John Lancaster
Peter Lane
John Lyons
Ian McMillan
Cheryl Martin
Eleanor Maxted
David Morley
Les Murray
Dorothy Nimmo
Pascale Petit
Eva Salzman
Lemn Sissay
Joan Jobe Smith
Martin Stannard
Mandy Sutter
Dennis Travis
Mary Woodward
Cliff Yates

For details of all our publications, and the current Competition, send an sae to The Poetry Business, The Studio, Byram Arcade, Westgate, Huddersfield HD1 1ND